I0531753

MONAD+MONADNOCK

Karen Donovan

Wet Cement Press
Berkeley, California

ISBN: 979-8-9856206-5-8

Wet Cement Press
1908 Yolo Ave
Berkeley, CA 94707

www.wetcementpress.com

Acknowledgments

Cover illustration by Karen Donovan.

"Not a Conspiracy, Not an Accident" makes use of some words of W. H. Auden.

The part-opening epigraph for "Monad" is from G. W. Leibniz, *Principles of Nature and Grace Based on Reason* (Jonathan Bennett, trans.). The part-opening epigraph for "Monadnock" is taken from Ralph Waldo Emerson's poem "Monadnoc."

Many thanks to the editors of these journals in which these poems first appeared:

Bryant Literary Review: "Dress Rehearsal for Utopia"; *Redactions*: "Kale"; *Conduit*: "Swung Dash," "For This Dish It Is Necessary That the Lobsters Be Alive,"

"Sharks," and "Trust Flees a Judge"; *Diode*: "Please Get Me My Godling Nebulizer" and "Throw the Deadbolt, Darlene"; *Eleventh Muse*: "I Love to Stand on the Backs of the Turtles" and "Of Her Tropism"; *Flights*: "Bat in the Lab," "Mack's Liver Mush," "Plex," and "Wild Type"; *The Germ, A Journal of Poetic Research*: "Aleph Naught," "Hypothesis 6," and "Parsimonious"; *Inter|Rupture*: "This Were My Fair Haven"; *Nedge*: "A Clarification" and "Life at KOA"; *Nice Cage*: "Mix It Up," and "Planetary Gearset"; *Saint Katherine Review*: "Hypnopompic"; *Spiral Orb*: "Viral"; *The Massachusetts Review*: "Clot"; *The 2River View*: "Story of an Origin" and "Orient."

Many thanks also to Dara Barrois/Dixon, who offered valuable feedback on previous versions of this book.

Twenty-two poems published here are included in a chapbook titled *Exploded Assembly*, which won the 2019 Sow's Ear Poetry Review chapbook contest.

Contents

MONAD

Because the world is full, everything in it is linked

PARSIMONIOUS

I left with a little stick in my hand.
It seemed right.

I'd been dreaming about straw,
the dry, dry plains of Potemkin.

When I woke the curtains were flaming artistically.
Amazing now to discover all this

reducible to a single theory: stroke deficit.
An old and elegant solution,

though unreconstructed, somewhat reminiscent of
add water—fill to brim.

Nevertheless my presumptions strode
masterfully down the block.

"Each caplet gets its own egg cup," I cried.
It was pitiful.

Mix It Up

Our leader sat under the sun.
She had a gun pinned to her lapel

and held a sheaf of wintergreen in her right hand.
In her left a scalp of unknown origin.

Her throne was of purest gold.
You'll note from the look in her eye

she was wishing for a cushion.
The landscape was indeterminate, a lake,

a banyan or two, a few courtiers unscrolling scrolls.
One began, "Be it so known…"

Skimming another, "…devastated by your silence."
The pull-down menu lists many more options.

That's me in the lower foreground
figuring in sand.

ALEPH NAUGHT

I wondered, are we addressing a collection of
the so-called infinite? A bag with the world in it

plus anything is still the same bag. Half a bag
with the world in it is equal to the whole bag.

Georg Cantor, it was too early in the century
for this, your idea Poincaré predicted would be

a disease from which one has recovered.
Shoulder to shoulder the cardinal numbers stood

like baby bottles vanishing forever into one-point
perspective, but you kept claiming, a bag's a bag,

forget the bottom! I'm not counting, stop counting!
Later they packed you off to the funny farm,

safe house for mathematics R&D, free
room and board. Nonetheless you were glum,

murmuring to the inmates, the material's all around, stack
it right, everything comes out even.

The principle was simple, just matching, your toes
with eternity's. We thought we could live without it.

CLOT

They'll say you can't, not with that
predicament on your face.

The phrase bus pulled up with another headline:
"Paris, 24 hours," and oh we were both

so happy watching pigeons in the Rossio,
being understated with our suitcases.

Remember those waitresses?
Those itinerant jewelrymongers eyeballing us

on street corners? In Cascais the sardines
were convincing. You yourself were

piquant by the bay. Golly, I'm terrified
by this box spring I'm about to own,

offbeat on the phone, dissembling with the movers.
When they ring I sit too still, aching to be out.

TRUST FLEES A JUDGE

So we nicked the keys to his Beemer.
So we floated his cockatiel.

Can't you folks take a joke?
It's the laugh track, Bugsy, I'm telling you,

narcotic substitution for the real
flashing marquees in everyone's brains

while the body's own sweet sugar
stands there with a candle.

Either that or a new motto:
Property is heft. I rest my case.

Now that we're breeding tomatoes
for sanguine inclinations, perhaps a lesson

on your own gene sequences? You can be replaced
without ever knowing. You're gone.

Taking the Open World Test

Please answer as completely and concisely
as possible. You are being timed.

A whistle floating by the window
Doppler-shifts Cole Porter.

I line up my three Ticonderogas side to side,
thinking *a segment of orange stockade fence.*

This booklet may include for experimental use
questions that have no correct solution.

You may begin.

TECHNOSTRESS

You wanted to say the day had broken,
to flee into some kind of excess.

No one was bleeding, for the moment.
No one was begging for a handful of corn.

Why wasn't this the paradisiacal extent?
Why wasn't this the cat's pajamas?

If we could minimize the elemental bizz-buzz,
if we could bathe in this blue haze forever.

The baby modems swing in their neural nets
database : database : database : database

You wanted to say the day had broken,
you wanted that sort of extravagance.

My Caryatid

Was always mistaken for a man,
her great ham hands and unshaven calves,

her set gaze, her obvious lack of wings.
No one knew where she had come from

and she liked it that way. Her duty:
to let the other women tend the goats,

to contemplate undisturbed her billion tiny globes.
She would not be opening her robe.

Through windows the moon scattered coins
of archipelagos across the floor,

every island a flawless stepping stone.
She sang the music each world would make

bouncing down the marble stair, its echo,
its spectrum, its cloudy air, its spin.

Hypothesis 6

A crane operator working parabolas out in his mind.
A few surrendering robins. A nickel heads up.

Interferonic dreams, the other side to sideless.
A moth that flies out, in, out of a room

like a moth, like beauty itself, mothlike, beautiful.
A moon that leans all its weight away,

an adolescent stripe we keep forgiving it for.
There's also a confident expanse of water.

The Hot Pile was a good name for Fermi's baby,
accelerating under the west bleachers

the colder that year got. I still like to say it: pile.
I woke up and I was you, persuasive as tide,

if you can imagine instead a constant avalanche,
an orange repeeling itself off the plate in a spiral,

one kid running the bases both ways,
as if and is as if and is as if and is.

LOOSE UP ROADS

So you put in, not to drift crosscurrents that meet
idle seams below snags, but to wake

mist-smoked, to dodge the sweeping estimations
of scheming bats, to watch the unfurling fiddleheads,

a stand of skunk cabbage, defiant
and odoriferous in black muck.

Swift by turns, a certain volume of river
moves you. The pines succeed each other thickly

or break to buzzing meadows
or slate cliffs that shed layers with spring floods,

and it's not what you see that isn't enough
or even that you see too much,

it's land swinging long a low fence line out past
turnings, deep clearings here, under your feet.

FOR THIS DISH IT IS NECESSARY THAT THE LOBSTERS BE ALIVE

Scallops shrimp breadcrumbs sherry.
Their swimmerets twitch.

It's not about the bodies. A study reveals
we can't hold on to events at all, that memory

flashbulbs night into day, shuffling the chairs
and losing the weapon in a welter of certainty.

In studio we build blue-gilt mirror glass, a single
globe per day. Nonetheless the bombing endures.

Gestures float in a dark room, too misty to see much:
American Rug in neon at the end of an off-ramp.

Hey, in these pics you've got dragon eyes.
What do you want? I was there.

SHARKS

Your lovely genitals—hell, they went first,
back with the inaugural tray of deviled eggs.

That surprised look on your face
as you offered up your right leg, then your left

and began bobbing in the conversation.
Still you waved one way and then the other,

refusing to be upended. Could you be mine?
I waited, over by the palms and the fleurs-de-lis,

flaunting my dance card, hanging on in the stiffening.
Save me your hands, I whispered.

BAT IN THE LAB

Whose eye spotted it first
banking around the Vandercook?

We'd been discussing Frederic Goudy, I believe,
hustling each other over his famous diamond-dotted i

and in other ways behaving like sages.
I was wearing my favorite shirt, so you

threw off your own and went after it. Would it bite?
It scrambled in the sack, blind as a bean,

then folded itself in the elevator going down
into a perfect origami replica of my heart,

one brown vest pocket hankie.
Off, off it went into the violet sky.

KALE

Was it his aftershave? He was always so hinky,
what my great-aunt called *a bad shoe*.

Inevitably, small animals died whenever
                                        his name came up.
Each night I pounded my brow for a ceremony,

recalling all that time under the same roof,
the silly balloon game he loved.

I did get an equation on the tip of my tongue.
It tasted like lace.

OF HER TROPISM

What's harder than not wanting
to surface at last?

She says *every line follows the length of its desire*.
She says it the way trees kneel in gray shifts

and peel their leaves off the sky,
how surf curls under and over again.

She says *first things as they come*,
watches a bee patrol the ceiling

and ocean bend in an arc that travels the curve
of far and near destinations,

but what moves her is always away from light,
deeper than seems a reasonable detour,

to a track in grass going out past laundry
pulling itself in wind.

LIFE AT KOA

I've seen that laundry waltzing in the yard,
the night ablaze with what we know

they look like, their shadows anyway,
all the nucleotides lamplit, taking their clothes off

in each tent, zipping, unzipping.
Something about its fluid quality,

about space so different it has its own alphabet.
At the playground until midnight kids

swing in their pajamas. Our little houses glow
along the riverbank like party lights.

I Love to Stand on the Backs of the Turtles

Night opens the oaks above me, above a bench where
a man rolled in a coat is dreaming the acorns are stars.

Across the square, water falls into a dish of pebbles.
Acorns drop in sparks.

The man sleeps under newspapers.
As he breathes, the prices of stocks rise and fall.

Water falls from bronze turtles with hooked jaws,
each tail a spiked curl. Two pike leap from a globe.

No cupids. Beneath the leaves the oaks let go of,
this man dreams. His lover's breasts are moonlit

apples he climbs to touch, and as he falls
he cries and knows he is awake. I walk in leaves.

The acorns are moons stamped by streetlights.
I love to stand on the backs of the turtles while water

falls into water and the pool never fills and
never empties. I carry my house, my four red rooms,

to the edge of a pool of circles of water,
this city, all clear to the bottom.

I Go Down to Cazenovia Lake to Read Chinese Poetry and Fall In

Like that other time.
My jeans steamed dry on the hood of our car

as I watched my father and brother pull trout
from the pond, the bad-tempered tongues of my boots

in the sun going *aaaaah*.
The one stone, Li Po says, always out of reach.

He looks up, inkbrush poised,
his face a mist of bamboo leaves,

his mind like the sand.
Not like that time,

I hang my socks on a branch,
struck silly in the chill of late fall.

A white gull flies, leaf boats dip and curl.
I don't have to go home at all.

Planetary Gearset

Well it must be angels, maybe racks and pinions
pitching instructions along gear to gear

to gear to gear, et voilà, complex revolution.
I cruise the suburbs looking for a cutaway view.

Suns rings bodies cogs. Prosaic perhaps,
but down here looks like a whole lot of spinning

with more or less torque, a mechanism that's not
                                    the latest
paradigm. Somebody's work keeps getting done.

Held parts make a hub, other parts revolve.
Come on, hang in. Hand to hand.

Give it some heart.

Mack's Liver Mush

You cried, Get away from me!
It was another, I don't know,

hardacre parking lot in West Virginia.
All I could think about was last night's salad bar,

squirrelly chickpeas, beets in their beety juice.
The road was a sine wave, undulating.

We bounced along in our yellow truck,
one swallowtail half-pasted to the windshield.

You'll get a ticket, parked like that!
Couldn't you see it was you I loved?

Across the hollow a tiny man swung
on his porch watching the pumps.

Tomorrow will come Tomorrow will come
We shared a root beer at the next Texaco.

Parallel Play

If you look out there a little to the west
you can see how the land drops off.

But the veining on this leaf?
It might put one in mind of a river delta.

I was thinking about the idea of branch water anyway,
the tinkling multicolored goblets of the demimonde.

∎

Here is the spigot and here is the sprocket.
Over the bay the cormorants...

Well, I wouldn't want to comment on that just yet.
But if I had been there, I'm sure I wouldn't have been.

Anyone could see he was a Java sparrow in disguise.
He blinked his bedroom eyes.

MEGAPLEX

I was becoming impatient.
My report was due and we were still on the first floor.

The next wallah played a repeating game:
"I've Got Bits of Fig in My Teeth."

Say, wasn't that an early piece
by Yoko Ono?

"Amplitude into blue sky" was the dessert.
People were throwing pennies into the potted palms.

It's a wishing witch, you said, hoping to delight me.
The light was implacable.

PLEX

In the midst of arriving babies
I paused to watch the swans

snipping up green plants in the lagoon
then drifting, heads tucked, on the tide.

Another binkie floated by...
I lassoed and pulled him in.

Tethered there the babies jostle in the wind
like balloon bouquets. The strings of course confuse.

Many administrators are now needed
to figure out whose is whose.

Such is history, woodbine and bittersweet,
sang the swans, asleep.

WILD TYPE

I thought: quick! jump in the elevator!
A little something between floors.

The laboratory zipped up tight, protecting
its expensive hybrids from off-road procreation.

Oh, look, you said. Forget the sex.
Let's get intense instead, build some rockets.

I looked up and noticed God was winking
from his trapeze.

He grabbed his own ankles.
His spangles were death-defying.

SWUNG DASH

Here was a machine I could almost date.
Switch number one sold the tango,

switch seven the cha-cha.
The keyboard was too much, daddy,

giving me third thoughts about today's possibilities,
and it wasn't even lunch.

I called back all my lost molecules
with more conviction than Patsy Cline.

The neighbors were having trouble
with renegade sterling,

but I was beyond them by then,
far across the ocean, doffing my little acorn cap.

UNDERGROUND ECONOMISTS IN ACCORD

Wow, this joint is packed.
Exactly. We love the client contact.

Ceramic ashtrays, an infinity of straight chairs,
lilies, right next to subpoenas.

Did you see the aisle signs?
Oblanceolate-Passerine-Somniferous

People can't photosynthesize: that's his business plan.
And shoppers keep asking for the moon

they say he promised,
all those waterfalls, fields of wild carrot,

dragonflies. Remember insects?
Here's a thermos, lightly used.

Oh, you first-timer, cry your eyes blue.
Empty your pockets as you pass through.

VIDEO REPLAYS

Attempts to bend the universe to do one's will may
not work. Cleaning a supply closet brings line cook
                                   face to face with reality.

School buses conspire to trap desperate commuter.
Beach rocks compete to get picked up.

People fail at yoga but still feel good about it.
Pineapple orange blueberry ginger smoothie
                              beats one hour of therapy.

Dog walker discovers body stretched out
on park bench is not a dead person. Some people
                              don't take a good picture.

Churchgoer bets one absence won't count too much
against her. Best way home is not a straight line.

▪

Visitors arrive underdressed and after curfew.
Desire will not stay buried.

Husband's hearing loss leads to amusing household
misunderstandings. Woman listens to the cosmos speak
                              but doesn't wish to mention that.

Last slice of pizza tries to avoid being eaten. Wind
blows leaves and papers around artfully in the street.

Incredible Hulk ruins another set of perfectly fine
clothing. Detective stares at computer screen,
                              then strikes a single key.

Books choose their own readers and are
remarkably picky about it. Dalmatian riding shotgun
                              endures opera CDs.

NOW THAT THE WORLD IS
NO LONGER STRANGE

I hang up by their laces my punch-drunk hands.
I hang them up and leave them swinging

against the wall like shadows,
like hands pretending to be birds.

Now that the world is no longer strange
I scroll my limbs into two dimensions

and become the ribbon and a traveler
who takes the ribbon.

I set my foot on the ribbon.
The world rises before me,

a stone seraph weeping and sniggering.
The tears are real, everything is real.

I give the stone my face to dissolve
the way gasoline contorts and colors and streams

rainbows in gutters.
I find I need my face no longer.

The flowers are real, the vipers are real.
Creation is singing.

MONADNOCK

Ages are thy days,
Thou grand expressor of the present tense

DAY AND NIGHT, AFTER ESCHER

Heaven chuckles at a trick that defeats
space and time so handily: two towns, a landscape

finite but unbounded. From here we see how it's done.
A traveler lays her past upon this world

like a template, finds a pattern roughly repeats
positive negative. Squared fields notch and melt

to vees of geese, one black wedge honking above town,
one white, fleeing toward evening.

The mirror doubles west and east a bridge, anti-bridge.
The traveler stands her ground, hearing the flock brush

between her and Corona Borealis, raising and tilting
her hand as a visor, wondering, is she her own twin

or is there another like her who so exactly misfits
her life? It is not known what at present prevents the sun

from appearing twice, what provokes these geese
reliably to fly into their barely plausible sky.

BRACKET THE SPEAKER

In order to come when called, the one addressed
must notice something particular about himself.

This morning he is thinking about the boxwood hedge
and how it wanted trimming.

But it isn't the hedge so much or that oddness lodged
in a place in his chest he once associated with love.

The weather seems directly aimed
at a spot adjacent to where he is standing.

He has expected news from a coastal village.
He has been warned not to divulge his secrets.

He has paused in the street trying to think of a name.
Like a rush into his mind, the hedge

and his wife of many years and a son who died at home.
And this matter of crossing a street at noon

in the company of a small sweet voice, a one-eyed girl
seated on a milk crate, playing a song.

People pat their jackets for change as they saunter by.
He decides the hedge can wait.

A message is imminent from a border town
he has never heard of.

In order to come when called, the one addressed
must notice something particular about himself.

NOT A CONSPIRACY, NOT AN ACCIDENT

She stands up and says, *make some trouble.*
Looks out at Manhattan, go on, go down to Mississippi.

And now you bring up that word, *tocsin*,
a stain, a spreading, a pealing of bells.

He stands up and says, *shove that job,*
do you believe in rock and roll?

Outside the civic center it's way below zero,
but inside, the groundlings' faces shine like stage lights.

People I want you
to put your hands together

A few arrests, quelled disturbances in neighboring blocks.
Coincidental beachgoers pause over their peach pits:

What was that? Reports come in from the body politic.
Something is going to fall like rain and it won't be flowers.

DRESS REHEARSAL FOR UTOPIA

We're glad they made Clear Falls.
The white rocks love the water,

the water loves its splash and brim.
Over the cliffs roll kids, kicking

with frogs in the beetled pools.
The bees crash-land in sticky nests.

We love our skin and the skin of others
under the sky that keeps nothing out.

A man goes wading, wearing a hat.
There's sand and a rusted bridge,

a gesture dark where the spring flowers.
A branch trails in pollen dust

hieroglyphics for minnows,
and the killer whales surrender

their air with grateful sighs
and flatten for the long ride home.

STORY OF AN ORIGIN

About how in the beginning it was
strong yet viscoelastic with certain properties

that distinguished it from sheet metal.
About how you can walk out on it
                                    for ice fishing in January.

About how it flows when warm like asphalt.
O how light it was.

Which made it advantageous for aerospace applications.
Hallelujah how there was no darkness in it

because we had had enough of that.
About how it made everything

except for everything that wasn't since there isn't
anything else than what keeps on getting

made and remade from ingredients the experts dispute.
About how nonlinearly it iridescently was

hard to predict with a tendency under load to deform
as worms grow wings, hillsides implode, bones rattle up

from rotor-whipped sands and begin to sing like flutes
about how in the beginning it was.

ORIENT

Heel prints of men and cattle
mark the ground at the watering place.
The mean wanders from center point.
I love you I love you I love you please.

At the watering place
men and cattle wander.
Look I'll mark the ground:
here is where we'll meet. Right here.

Scores wander off the curve.
Fresh prints of men and cattle, filling with snow.
I know you can find it, it's on the map.
The map is a map. There is a forest. There is a steppe.

There is a watering place.
Point line plane solid hypersolid.
Angle radian perimeter sphere, cherubim seraphim.
Men and cattle, later a panther.

Find Sirius Rigel Aldebaran.
Horizon. Tabletop doorstep road.
Orchil sunset. Sweet fig. Tracer bullets.
The woodsmoke the slipknot the clove.

Boolean Yoga

Wants to be murdered by love,
keeps falling into wellness.

Avoids rearranging the furniture,
decides to draw squares on paper.

Dreads lemon fluorescence,
believes in horse bristle.

Believes in being murdered by love,
wants to fall into wellness.

Keeps painting the corner last,
avoids falling into wellness.

Decides on lemon fluorescence,
decides to rearrange the furniture.

Avoids obeying instructions,
dreads horse bristle.

Dreads drawing squares on paper,
keeps being murdered by love.

Believes in lemon fluorescence,
dreads being murdered by love.

Believes in painting the corner last,
keeps drawing squares on paper.

Avoids lemon fluorescence,
wants to rearrange the furniture.

Wants an aspergillum.
Settles for horse bristle.

A CLARIFICATION

Your question if we are hearing it correctly
is what to do with personal death.

Give away, give away the gift.
The proton has been shown experimentally

to be stable for 10^{32} years. Still.
Lullaby, construct creation myths that amuse,

please also to soothe archaic terrors
in the bulge at the end of the brain stem.

My son, my daughter, this has all happened.
Right, but do we make of it...

Assume we've reconsidered the colors
of dawn. In fact, avoid color.

A word. You imagine a word remains.
Get a grip. Have kids or go

into business, something steady
and useful maybe: materials science:

permutate, combinate. I've poured
the periodic table into a few molds myself, love,

the experiment kills you repeatedly until you get it right.
That's when they accuse you of fudging your data.

Part of you stands apart, coolly watching
as you blather on the witness stand.

We are going down that river.
A sparrow bangs the windowpane.

No! Wait!
I can explain.

VIRAL

The difference between dust and
bittersweet flaming the treetops.

Constant the having to reinvent.
The its being so leaky.

Meanwhile a rabid skunk
is dying in the geraniums.

Blooms near total aphasia.
The difference between dust and

pattern computing in my thumbprint.
Pi the music the bittersweet flaming.

Near total eclipsing its leaky.
Pink lingering after the truck bombs.

The getting and staying off zero,
the getting.

After the truck bombs
the difference between zero and

here
shivers the plus and minus.

Skunk mind,
fever mind.

Won't you eat.
Won't you eat something.

PLEASE GET ME MY GODLING NEBULIZER

Our ideas were terrible and we were all at fault,
snapping our brains like dust mops
at every passing airfoil, taking subtraction lessons

from the nation's biggest meniscus.
It's like a drive-by backbone-ectomy,
mumbled the undercoat in line ahead of me.

We retaliated with mass visualization, drew up chairs,
placed our hands palms down on the tabula rasa
and sweated visual purple.

A wheatear's tenderness witnessed to my throat.
My neighbor confessed to ordering fairy shrimp
in kingcup, to thermic doo-wop in the shower,

to wishing his extremities would juvenesce.
We were breathing in rivulets, entering zona pellucida
without broadband coverage,

but when we opened our uncials the world
was still here, and a quorum of malefactors
were making off with the jollyboats,

a vexatious anticlimax, as a famous hymnologist
in an infamous sentence once called an extraneous *Amen*.

THROW THE DEADBOLT, DARLENE

It is my shift at The Bureau.
I step in wearing an oilcloth coat,
yank my key from the lock.

One hallway bulb glows peachlike
in midair then fails the imitation.
It is a night I dream of my father,

whom I miss now more than ever.
My best friend departs the territory,
carrying enough seed to start over.

At dinner, none of the hotplates will work.
Periwinkles gleam in a faraway bay.
Our children witness indelible events,

a few umbrellas blow out.
Still we seek a faithful copy of reality,
right down to the make-believe ending.

We offer the prisoner an airy suite,
fresh tacks for his hands and his feet.
We tie prayers in strips torn from our shirts,

the shirts we were reportedly born in.
So I do know which desk it is.
My chair is already warm.

SOME DEMISEMIQUAVERS

The acquiesce : the bandbox
    the banished : the castanet

The catacomb : the drunktalk
    the decapod : the endlong

The fabulist : the featherstitch
    the gnomon : the hula

The interrupt : the jigsaw
    the jetblack : the keystroke

The leatherback : the leafhop
    the magnificat : the nondescript

The one-two : the pretext
    the quintuplicate : the rare earth

The sibyllic : the tailwash
    the ultrasound : the venomous

The winnow : the why not
    the xed-out : the yaw

THE OYSTER LISTENER

He admires bats.
When panic hits, he stands in a doorway.

He decodes your end from your beginning.
If methylated, he gets intoxicated.

On weekends, he is enlightened by your doubts.
He calls you by accident when you feel erasable.

The tide was never his friend.
Occasionally he leaves the planet

carrying only a small valise.
No one would guess he is homeless.

"A cryptic appearance conceals a lepidopteran"
is an acrostic for his prayer.

Where Words Began

There was music.
We lay in dust at the crossroad,

it was warm, the road was lined with seashells.
Gulls in orbits above.

We did not speak, our tongues were too heavy.
The earth and all the planets were turning at once

and we knew this. The design was in it.
When you rose from your sleep I counted five stars.

And there was a music abroad,
blue myrtle, growing through stones.

Will I again take your hand in the morning?
I look down the long coil and hear the ocean,

combing and combing.
The blue myrtle, until you return.

FOR ONE CRAZY-ASS MINUTE ANYWAY

It struck: a tiny cyclone of thought: my legacy
would be numismatic, a jangle-jingle
                                        in the pockets of giants.
I was eating red licorice at the laundromat,
reading about trinitarianism, Zoroastrianism,
Aztec human sacrifice. My jeans backed up into rinse.

From behind the counter our evening attendant
chuckled into his cell phone like a partridge:
She should have cited that source.

What source, and who was she?
But when I looked around, every eye was locked
                                        on a dryer port
in multidimensional continuous partial attention.
No one noticed that corporations were greenwashing
their resumes, that action steps needed to be taken.

I have waded by accident into a mating dance
of miner bees. I have sworn emotional attachment
to reality, specifically at a campsite in Ohio,
in a dark event involving a tent. To wit:
I could see it was a williwaw, a word I have vowed
                                        never to use.
It stirred the verticals and was gone.
I went back to my book.

THIS WERE MY FAIR HAVEN

That I do not wish to obey, I admit.
My hat flaps on its peg like a half-dead moth.

Oh, how I wish to quit the claustral parlor
of this popup camper and go out to greet those

harder, darker objects of my solace,
the sky, for example, hung with a double moondog

tonight, and every last ember sputtering
back at us since the beginning of time.

The door bangs shut from all illumination.
Offered a pillow, I will decline.

Then I can stand in our street like other mute oaks
and observe your pantomime, awaiting that

wayward lurching of heart from intrepidity to dread,
squeezing a stone in my hand and willing my soul

true. I can exhale again a drift of white mist.
I can drop to one knee and yield

while a man dressed in linen draws with a bone
of warm charcoal across my brow the taw

and a girl on a bike with no headlamp wildly
rounds the corner, late, bound for somewhere else.

Ars Poetica Update

I spend too much time on kiloparsecs.
I forget to exhale.

I plod the avenue of palmy afternoon encumbered
                                        by the zeitgeist.
I watch my idiot narrative feet.

I strike the checklist and make a pancake landing
                                        on deck.
I divide by interpupillary distance: whoops.
I letter in demotic veronica.
I leave by the kitchen exit.

■

Have given up control of my verbs.
Am feeling bottom of soapy basin for fork.

Not as though nothing matters
but does: but in its own timeframe.

Have admitted zoological origins.
Am now presuming no innocence.

Not as though history were over
but some damn thing in there ticking.

.

The garden: everything that wants to and does.
Wild bean tangles with willow.

Dragonfly whirrs by fast slow fast.
Stirs its tiny robot body and swivels many eyes.

Stars, invisible as usual.
Swans, majestic and opinionated.

A hand moves to draw what is
already perfect in my head.

So I Displayed a Fearless Iotacism

(i)
I leveled my top hat and took up with the countess,
I licked my finger and drew her likeness in sugar,
I snapped my pluperfect suspenders into the next
dimension, I vanished like Cornish.

(ii)
I got free drinks from a lethal gene behind the bar,
I finished my meal despite his pecuniary stare,
I eulogized licorice, I quoted Lawrence on
hummingbirds: "Lions no bigger than inkspots!"

(iii)
I fingered the sore spot of my providential splinter,
I picked through green beans like a turnstone,
I shook out my shoes and shouted at the sandbur,
I spread my solar sail and set a course for Cygnus.

(iv)
I mimed "glockenspiel" out a side window, I passed
through Akron, I stole the heel of a previous loaf,
I felt the felt and it felt good.

(v)
I heard that chemotaxis was a matter of aesthetics,
I welcomed that thought, I crawled into a lode
of primordial lead, I tracked lentissimo to its lair.

(vi)
I laid a kitchen whisk to my mackled past, I dedicated
my days to diffusion and my nights to viscous drag,
I assessed the caterpillar overplus, I collected "cat
sneeze" in 46 languages.

(vii)
I argued in vivo vs in silico before a kangaroo court,
I insisted on ephemerids, I feted the animalcule expert,
I wanted her mesocarp to be my mesocarp.

(viii)
I rhymed *soccer moms* with *cherry bombs*, the trouble was:
those shrubs were increasingly tussive, I desired to take
him at his word, the trouble was: he had no word.

Exasperated Midrash I

The more you read, the harder it is not to notice.
A woman making decisions always seems to wind up

soaked in the blood of some relative.
A moment of deliberation. Of weakness?

Meantime the guys boing-boing an abstract
shuttlecock, slipping knee-deep in brains.

Somebody on the payroll wheelbarrows out the bodies.

This one had a choice.
Why not consider John the Baptist's head on a plate?

Why not second-guess goggle-eyed Herod, ready to cede
half the kingdom to a topless girl waving a veil?

How could he make a promise like that?
Take it! Whatever! It's yours!

Exasperated Midrash II

I slammed my own heart in the door as I left.
No, really, I'm okay, I'm fine!

Regarding martyrdom, raise your hand
if you identify most with the ram caught in a thicket.

We felt that sinking feeling as Abraham approached,
relief and conviction gleaming on his brow like the sun.

Uh-oh.

And the desert burned the story to its outline.
Why this day? Why this man and this boy

and this awfully sharp blade?
The lessons never cease. Dear whomever,

whomsoever, one blunder and you win the prize,
at least in this tale about sacrifice.

Scientists Surprised at Persistence of Urchin Barrens

Such was the age when lovers
of God were misanthropes,
lovers of humanity unelectable,
and all allegory ironic

for the sake of deniability.
Let's imagine something
we can't kill, *Staphylococcus*
perhaps or that army of echinoderms

chewing at the Pacific coast,
so simple, so ancient,
with an immune system to die for,
pentamerous radial symmetry

directing design for
this jeweler's case of a skeleton
and circlet of five incisors.
Sea urchins set forests of kelp

adrift just eating lunch,
spurt aquanaut babies that pop
into spheres and colonize rocks.
Heaving in spiky pillows and hillocks,

the benthos waves from its acreage
a vast lawn of aerials synchroed
to tide, sprawls on glazy
sucker feet like epic simile.

Absurd, since you can split one
with a whack, I've heard,
quick snack for otters when
there were otters, such was the age.

YOU'LL NEED YOUR SEABOOTS
FOR THIS

When the weather turns left I'll turn into it,
reaching for washouts with my inherited pedipalps,
wagering grapeshot precision I can get home
before lightning thumbtacks me to the palisades.

My middle game has never been that great,
a lame excuse, so I will always forget your birthday
but ontically be present for the moment of your death.
You've left me, a yearling stranded nohow in tansy.

Later, as the executrix unbuttons your testament,
you'll rise for us lustrous and soaking wet
with the oatcake of peace on your tongue.
I remember the sun like upholstery in the afternoon,

espièglerie in the top rigging, roving quintillions
of buttery krill. *Will a minnow be my drayman?*
I hope so. And jacinth your first chandler,
my knight-errant, my impresario, my camelopard.

I should have returned at once but for the tide.

LOOK, THAT'S A XEBEC ON THE HORIZON

Once a squat line of ducks appeared around the corner
I relaxed. Situation: normalized.

The cove? The cove I suppose was tranquil,
but the stove was aboil.

I was making sorbet the wrong way.
A voice from offstage: You always do that.

It was the pin tumbler.
He was about to gain entry.

The pipes hooted, the TV blazed.
I tried to remember my lessons:

insert, align, rotate, click!
Look deeeep into my eyes.

A perfect little mechanism operating perfectly
with very little sweat.

The Rental Agent

It was too hot, and some of us were having
a luckier time of it than others.
Across the café, unhinged, a dispute about lilacs.

Vacancies, he groaned, so rare, so rare, the prices...
I offered currency, my best pebbles, which he took
and plunked one by one over the boxwood hedge,

widening haloes of ripple on the duck pond.
I think he was aiming at the ducks.
Consider this an investment in our relationship.

He handed me the catalogue, but the page I chose
disappointed him. Really? Taffeta?
He pursed his lips, adjusted his green eyeshade.

The lease on that is forty years. I was about to ask
if it would be long enough, but he was already
signaling the waiter like a third-base coach.

Then, hunting crumbs, two sparrows
lit on the sidewalk, the envy of all.
Those... I don't suppose... No, he replied,

instantly happier than I'd seen him all day.

You Know It As Toast

Six a.m. on the corner of Dwight and Worthington
every day but Sunday, which eliminates

brunchers, who can't get mimosas here anyway,
the cooks at Rick's flip on the grill and deep fryers

and arrange the licorice whips and Doritos
under the counter

and let in the early birds cooling their spike heels
across at the Silver Dollar Saloon.

It's an instant infusion of nonfiltered exhalations.
The ceiling fans don't work and everyone's

intently creating familiar environments
as fast as they can.

Glazed and a regular costs you a buck.
There's a picnic down the block: vinyl banners

trumpeting the miracle of private investment
to pregnant girls and goth punks

and transfer commuters trying to get to the malls.
The bran muffins are just for show.

Pick up, please!
Benny slaps his spatula, skids a platter past,

while the bricklayers, bug-sized on scaffolds
above Main Street, doubt the weather will last.

Hypnopompic

I had ordered my dodecahedrons,
the ones with creamy centers,
when my brain parted at the seam
and an apostrophe flew out.
It was a shy apostrophe, emerging

with reservations. Just like when
you came back from the auto junkyard
and said *it was aisles and aisles of Opels*,
an invisible shrine opened and shone
with instant snowblink on a backhoe

stopped at the drive-through,
catching me half-jounce, semi-late,
whelmed with experiments in spacetime.
My commute wavered at storm drains
and the knave in the Ford behind me

was behaving badly, darkling glints
of his efficiency in dentistry,
but I kept both hands on the wheel
and spoke it aloud to memorize,
Our lives are of infinite size.

A PIXEL

Of icy archetypes cored from the ancient blue poles,
of sodic mists driven cold off bleached seawrack,
of certain square inches in the lawn,

yes, I was slavish in my enthusiasms,
restless, pointillist, jumped by carmine at street corners,
my third eye going psychokinetic.

I framed the roof edge with a rhomboid of sky
and clicked, sought a pismire's vision of goosegrass
or hydrogen primes glued like garden snails to the rim

of the cosmos, blast craters, snake handlers,
babies on ponies. I dreamt up topology
for contiguous sheets then shook the mechanism out

to learn how my weird soul was laid
soft as a pillowcase painted with moonlight
across the surface of everything as if it were everything.

WHERE EACH BASE UNIT IS A SINGLE STRAND WITH INFINITE GIVE

What *Araneus diadematus* pulls from her spinneret
at dusk every night in my yard, a line extended between

two points from which the plane of existence suspends

my body, your body, the unimaginable shape to come,
where the spider answers her path, an urgent matter

of spokes arrayed and crossmembers knitted in
a spiraling labyrinthine return to the center—*there*.

One little winch like a tightened fist, then she steadies,
braced to catch whatever it is the dark has sent her.

MONAD+MONADNOCK

I zoom a kestrel as it swoops off
in the direction of the Water Bearer.

With our field glasses, we can see it all
from up here. My friend the critic

who switches lights on and out for a living
asks me if damson truly has an edible isomer,

if kestrels signify. "Doesn't the uncanny valley
still broil with the simulacra of empire?

Isn't this yammer and bristlecone
so much waxed paper?"

Her feet hurt from our climbing.
She wants her marmalade lunch.

I would draw my answer in longhand,
but what I've got is one parsnip.

If the endoplasmic reticulum knows more
than it's telling us, if voltaic zircon

can be reliably trained, if we unearth the index fossil
from this layer, if teasel/sargassum etcetera,

we will have more insight into *the neverending possible.*
"Pasta bowl," she objects. "He said

neverending pasta bowl, the guy on the TV."
As if that matters to me.

About the Author

Karen Donovan lives in Rhode Island, where she works in the nonprofit community as a writer and editor. She is the author of *Planet Parable* (Etruscan Press), which was published in an innovative multi-author volume called *Trio*. Her other books of poems are *Your Enzymes Are Calling the Ancients* (Persea Books), which won the Lexi Rudnitsky / Editor's Choice Award, and *Fugitive Red* (University of Massachusetts Press), which won the Juniper Prize. Her book of illustrated short prose, *Aardvark to Axolotl* (Etruscan Press), is a collection of tiny stories and essays inspired by the engravings in a vintage Webster's dictionary. From 1985 to 2005 she and co-editor Walker Rumble at Oat City Press published *¶: A Magazine of Paragraphs*, a print journal of very short prose. She is currently at work collaborating with her rock collection on a hybrid book of text and image.

.

www.ingramcontent.com/pod-product-compliance
Lightning Source LLC
Chambersburg PA
CBHW030509130626
46549CB00007B/2907

* 9 7 9 8 9 8 5 6 2 0 6 5 8 *